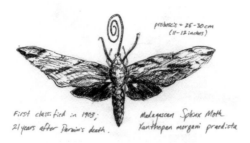

probosis = 25-30cm
(11-12 inches)

First classified in 1903,
21 years after Darwin's death.

Madagascan Sphinx Moth
Xanthopan morgani praedicta

Charles Darwin
and His R*EVOLUTION*ary Idea

By Brian "Fox" Ellis
Illustrations by Peter Olson
© 2008
Fox Tales International
P.O. Box 10800
Peoria, IL 61612
www.foxtalesint.com

Based on the Writings of Charles Darwin:
The Voyage of the Beagle (1831-1836)
and The Origin of Species (1859)

ISBN: 1-4392-1636-3
EAN13: 9781439216361
Library of Congress Control Number: 2008909857

Acknowledgements: The Author would like to thank countless science teachers who have cheered him on; Brad Henz for designing this book; Peter Olson for his astounding use of color; his wife Kim Thrush, for her tough intellect; and Charles Darwin for his 30 years of research and persistence in pursuing his passion and beliefs.

The artist would like to thank Charles Darwin for contributing so much to the conversation between man and nature; Fox for inviting him into this particular project; Neil Colwell for providing design assistance and his wife Janean for being a constant source of inspiration and encouragement.

Imagine a cloudy overcast day in Darwin's library at his home in England. You have just arrived to spend an afternoon basking in the glow of this learned man. He has invited you to listen to the tales of his adventures circumnavigating the globe, sailing around the world on H.M.S. Beagle!

Welcome, welcome. So you have come to talk to me about my r*evolution*ary idea, evolution.

Please, please have a seat; could I offer you a spot of tea?

Where do I begin? With questions, of course! Questions are the foundation of all good science!

I spent my life trying to answer the big questions, the mystery of mysteries… Did creation happen just once? Or is the story of creation forever and always unfolding? Consider all of the creatures upon the earth today; were they all here since the dawn of time? Or do you believe that new species evolve from the old? If you believe as I do, how is it that new species are formed? What are the mechanisms by which species adapt to changes in the world around them?

In the struggle for survival, what governs the success of some and the extinction of others? What are the laws of nature that shape life upon this planet?

These are the questions I sought to answer and shall answer for you if you dare to ask.

Would you care for a scone or maybe a teacake to go with your tea?

I have always been fascinated with the diversity of life here on this planet we call earth. I have often wondered why there are so many different species of birds and beetles and bats and how all of these different species have come to be. My grandfather, Erasmus Darwin, wrote a book about evolution called "*Zoonomia*," so the idea isn't new, but his book was more philosophical than scientific, and he was scorned, laughed at, ridiculed. No one had answered the question about the mechanisms of change. How does evolution work? I spent my entire life, more than 30 years trying to work out the details.

My curiosity began as a young man. I was always wandering in the forest and fields of my Uncle Josiah Wedgewood's estate.

My research began when I was yet in college, at Edinburgh, Scotland, where I began to collect beetles in earnest. No poet ever felt more delighted at seeing his first poem published than I did at seeing my first beetle identified in Stephens' *Illustrations of British Insects;* under the illustration were the magic words, 'captured by C. Darwin, Esq."

I will not soon forget one afternoon in particular.

As I was walking along, I came upon a tree where some bark was peeling loose. There I spied a beetle. Without a net or collecting jar, I snatched it up in my hand. In almost the same moment I spied a second, distinctive beetle and snatched it up into my other hand. Soon after, under the edge of the bark, I saw a third unique species of beetle. What was I to do? Two hands, three beetles, I popped one beetle into my mouth to free up a hand. In that same instant the beetle squirted an acrid fluid into my mouth. My tongue, lips and the inside of my cheeks burned with this acidic fluid. What would you do? Exactly what the beetle would want you to do. You would spit out the beetle, as did I. The third beetle, the one I was about to scoop up also escaped.

I had to pause, and wonder… How could there be three *varieties* of beetles under this one piece of bark? Clearly, all three were insects, with their six legs and hard shiny, exoskeleton, but such variety in one small place? Each had *adapted* to different foods: One had pinchers for eating leaves, one had a snout for sucking sap, and one had larger pinchers for eating other beetles, an herbivore, a parasite and a carnivore. Over *time*, these species had changed to survive, *inheriting* traits from their ancestors, but what mechanism *selected* these species to thrive here?

I later transferred to Trinity College in Cambridge. At Cambridge, I brushed up on my Greek and Latin and Hebrew. I studied the Bible and church history, but I also took every course in Natural history that I could. I met J. S. Henslow, a professor of botany. I took all the courses he offered. I took one botany course three times. I became known as "The man who walks with Henslow". Professor Henslow used to say "What a fellow that Darwin is for asking questions!" Henslow challenged me to think about each species of plant and how it fit in the larger scheme of things.

Henslow introduced me to Reverend Adam Sedgewick, a geologist who allowed me to join him on a walk through Wales, a geological survey. This tour was of decided use in teaching me how to make out the geology of a country. He taught me to read the landscape like a book. The stones tell the stories of the history of the land. I was simply amazed at how he could piece together evidence from scattered clues! But the most important thing I learned from Professor Sedgewick was that science is more than a collection of facts, more than a collection of rocks or beetles or dried flowers. Science was a process of asking difficult questions and looking for answers. The facts are important, but science consists in grouping facts so that general laws or conclusions may be drawn from them.

Unbeknownst to me, all of this was preparing me for the journey of a lifetime. I must admit I was obsessed with the idea of travel and exploration, after graduating tenth in a class of 178, my head was running on about the Tropics. My enthusiasm was so great that I could hardly sit still. I had written myself into a tropical glow.

There is no doubt my fascination with beetles, barnacles and boulders led to my invitation to be the ship's naturalist for the H.M.S. Beagle. I was invited to spend what eventually became five years aboard this ship circumnavigating the globe. The word excitement does not begin to describe my feelings when I was asked to go along.

If someone asked you to sail around the world, would you say yes? Of course!

We left England on December 27, 1831. I could tell you a hundred stories about my travels. And, if you would like to learn more you may wish to read my book, *Voyages of Beagle*. Please allow me to share with you five short stories that led to my theory of evolution:

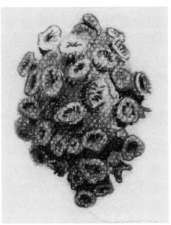

"Ñandu"

Greater Rhea
Rhea *americana*
125 - 140 cm (49-55") tall

dark "collar"
on male

both can
run at
60 km/hr.
(37 mph)

white
spots

Lesser "Darwin's" Rhea
Rhea *pennata*
90 - 100 cm (35 - 39") tall
Thicker feathers are an
adaptation to the colder
climate further south.

VARIATION

While the ship was in port, measuring the depths of the ocean, the bay, the inlet, and the rivers that flowed into the sea, I was ashore. This was the ship's mission, to make maps, so Her Majesty's Ships, HMS, could sail safely around the world, into and out of many ports. While the ship was in port, I spent most of my time exploring. I will never forget the first time I visited the rainforest of the Amazon Basin. I saw a beautiful winged jewel fluttering about, my first hummingbird, a bird that has no rival and no close relatives in England. My eyes followed it to an amazing flower, also new to me. My eyes followed the vine up to the tree on which it clung. The size and shape of the leaves were astounding. And, from another entwining vine bloomed a second type of flower. Then the flower seemed to take wing, no, it was a butterfly the size of a dinner plate! Everywhere I looked there was some new discovery!

Eventually I collected more than 10,000 specimens which I dried, preserved, dissected, and/or pickled to ship back to England. More than 2000 of these species were new to science.

One that still bears my name, Darwin's Rhea, is also known as the lesser rhea. The rhea is a large flightless bird similar to the ostrich of Africa and the emu of Australia. I had learned to hunt rhea while travelling with the gouchos on the plains of South America. I believe you would call these fellows cowboys. They taught me how to swing a rather unique implement made of three to five stones, bound in leather, attached to long strings, called bolos. The gouchos would whirl the bolos above their heads, and the momentum will carry the bolos some distance with deadly effect. The strings will entangle the legs of the large rhea and bring them down. The gouchos would then skin and eat the bird, rather much like a turkey. When I made my first attempt with the bolos, one of the rocks hit a branch overhead and instead of hurling out to catch my prey, the bolos tangled the legs of my horse. I was nearly thrown to the ground! I have never seen the gouchos laugh so heartily. They said it was the first time they had ever seen a hunter capture himself!

They told me of another smaller species of rhea that lived on these same plains, further to the south. We searched for weeks but never found one. Well, we did not find one until I was back aboard the ship.

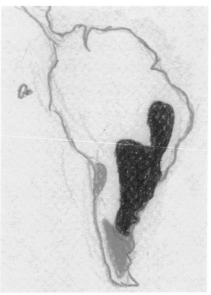

Charles Darwin and his *Revolution*ary Idea

A few weeks later we were sailing further south along the coast of South America. The cook had prepared a fine feast, for it was our Christmas dinner. There was a variety of fresh game from the shore and delicious seafood caught that morning as we sailed along. My favorite was the roasted rhea. My first thought was that this was an immature rhea. It was smaller than the ones I had eaten with the goucho. A smaller rhea! It was not until I had picked the bones clean and saw them arrayed on my plate that I realized I had discovered a new species! But, I had eaten it! I picked the bones from everyone's plates and pieced them together. Luckily for me, the skin had not yet been tossed overboard to feed the sharks that followed us everywhere the ship went. With the skin intact and a nearly complete skeleton, I had all the evidence I needed to name a new species, the lesser rhea.

But all of this begs the question: How could two varieties of basically the same bird inhabit different regions of the same plain? This *variation* on a theme: the ostrich, emu and rhea are all large flightless birds that have developed long strong legs to help them survive in a grassland environment. But, they are different species, unrelated; did they have a common ancestor and share inheritance? Or, are they unrelated and some factor in their common environment led to each bird developing similar traits? Why would two species, greater and lesser rhea, live in the same country?

Glyptodont - from the Greek word for "grooved tooth."

Glyptodonts probably weighed over 1000kg (2200 lbs.) and were up to 3m. (10 ft.) long.

Living during the Cenozoic Era of the Pleistocene Epoch, they became extinct about 10,000 years ago.

Their carapace was formed from hundreds of inch-thick armor plates called "osteoderms."

Pichi (Zaedus pichiy)

3-banded Armadillo (Tolypeutus matacus)

Lesser Fairy Armadillo (Chalmyphorus truncatus)

Armadillos belong to the order Xenarthra, along with sloths and anteaters.

INHERITANCE

While travelling with the gouchos, we often breakfasted on armadillos. (Maybe I should mention that in the five years I spent with the ship HMS Beagle, I spent more than 2/3rds of my time on shore). Surely you know the armadillo, a small hard shelled mammal who curls up in a ball for protection? We would cook them in their shell. Each armadillo was a fine breakfast for two men.

Maybe I should also mention that my brother still teases me, saying I fairly ate my way around the world. But when one is travelling in remote regions, you too would eat whatever was at hand! My brother also said, "Wherever Charles Darwin goes there will be a trail of mass extinctions… on his dinner plate!"

The gouchos took note of my interest in unusual creatures, so they took me to visit a friend who had a rather large armadillo shell. The shell was so large he used it as shelter for his young pigs! I asked where he found it. He took me to the spot, a cliff along the coast. There I found additional fossils of a prehistoric relative of the armadillo, the glyptodont. This ancient beast lived many thousands of years ago; I could tell because of the other fossils I found near it including the giant sloth bear. Did you know your President, Thomas Jefferson, was the first to describe the giant sloth bear? Megalonyx jeffersoni still bears his name. Well, the shell of this glyptodont was so large that you or I could wear it as armor! The sloth bear was so large it could pull down a tree to eat the tender leaves near the top.

Indeed, every discovery leads to more questions: How long ago did these giants roam the earth? Through inheritance what traits had been passed down to their now smaller descendents? What had the smaller modern armadillo inherited from its larger ancestor besides its shell? What did the smaller three toed sloth inherit from its largest ancestor besides an appetite for leaves in the tree tops? What is the span of time needed for such adaptations to take place?

Upheaval of Sedimentary rock

level of sea

Fossilized Coral

A B C D E F G H I J K L

island   level of sea

barrier reefs

Petrified Wood

TIME

Several months later we had sailed around Tierra Del Fuego, the land of fire that is the southern tip of South America. While there, we set ashore a few natives that our good captain had brought home to England on his last journey. He had tried to Christianize them but they quickly reverted to their tribal ways.

After we had found safe passage through Cape Horn and mapped a way for others to follow, skirted the Antarctic Ocean and began to head north along the west coast of South America, it was then we encountered a terrible earthquake!

It still grieves me to think of the town of Concepcion, completely flattened by the trembling earth. Even the large, sturdily built Spanish cathedral lay in ruins. The hovels of the peasants were a pile of rubble. We, the men aboard the ship, were spared, safe at sea. We did all we could to bring food and fresh water to the survivors on shore.

What amazed me was the way this earth's quake had tossed up a shelf of the coast line. Land that was yesterday a coral reef under water, the next day stood seven feet above sea level.

A few weeks later, while climbing up the side of the High Andes Mountains, we came across a forest of petrified wood, not a log or two, but acres and acres of an ancient forest that did not decay like wood today. The cells of the tree were replaced with minerals that turned the tree to stone, fossilized.

A few days after that discovery we climbed to the arid desert at the very top of the Andes Mountains. At the top of the mountains, 12,000 feet above sea level, we found sea shells, the fossils of a coral reef!

I must ask you to ponder this: How does land that was once a vast forest, fall beneath the sea to gather sea shells on top, and then this same landform rise 12,000 feet above sea level? Go ahead, answer this question for me…

You can do the mathematical computation: if the shelf of the sea floor can rise seven feet in one earthquake and such an earthquake happens maybe once every hundred years, how many millennia for the sea bottom to rise 12,000 feet? Add to this the number of years for a forest to fossilize and fall beneath the sea far enough to gather a coral reef on top!

Clearly, the earth is very old, much older than the Reverend Wilberforce would have us believe in his literal translation of the Bible. Do you know Wilberforce? He published a book that was quite popular claiming the earth was only 6,000 years old and that man and dinosaurs had inhabited the earth at the same time. Clearly, the processes of change of which I speak take millions and millions of years, not hundreds or even thousands. Great expanses of time are needed for the earth to change, for climates to change, and for the species of the earth to adapt to these changes.

I was so fascinated by these questions that I later wrote a book on the geology of the Andes Mountains and published the first color coded map of all of the types of stone from which these gorgeous mountains are made.

Galapagos Islands

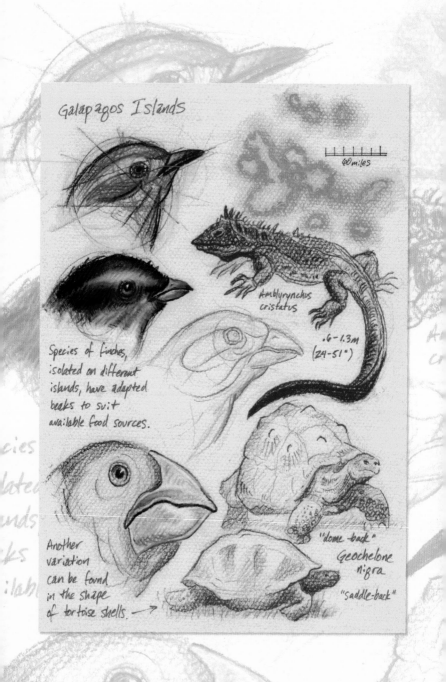

⌐⌐⌐⌐⌐⌐⌐
60 miles

Amblyrynchus cristatus

.6–1.3 m
(24–51")

Species of finches, isolated on different islands, have adapted beaks to suit available food sources.

Another variation can be found in the shape of tortoise shells. →

"dome-back"
Geochelone nigra

"saddle-back"

SELECTION & ADAPTATION

From the West Coast of South America we sailed to the now famous Galapagos Islands, a tiny group of volcanic islands that rise up out the depths of the Pacific Ocean where several unique ocean currents meet. What most struck me here was not the idea that there were hundreds and hundreds of new species, but that a handful of species had gradually adapted to the various islands in unique ways.

There were several different varieties of Galapagos Tortoises. The Governor told me he could identify which island a tortoise was from by the shape of its shell. Some were more round and others had a dip like a Spanish saddle. And yes, we did dine on tortoise meat. It was common practice for sailors to come ashore and replenish their supply of fresh water. While they were there, they would capture as many as a hundred of these 200 pound behemoths and keep them alive onboard ship so they would have fresh meat for months to come. These creatures could live for several months with no food or water. I understand that one of the tortoises we caught and delivered to Australia lived at a small zoo owned by a Mister Steve Irwin, which would make this tortoise more than 150 years old!

We also discovered a new species of iguana on the Galapagos, a marine iguana. Most iguanas are green, live in the tree tops and eat leaves. These marine iguanas were black so they could absorb heat from the sun and blend in with the black volcanic rocks. They had flattened tails for swimming. They had a special gland in their nose so they could absorb salt from the sea and blow it out the way you would blow snot from your nose. They were excellent swimmers and dined on seaweed and moss on the ocean floor. And yes, I did eat iguana and yes indeed, it does taste like chicken. Green Iguana is a common food in South America.

I once caught a marine iguana and tossed it into the sea to see how well they can swim. It crawled right back out onto the rock and looked at me like I was daft. I picked it up and tossed it again. It crawled right back out onto the same rock. It stared me down. I tossed it a third time and a third time it climbed back out. My first thought was, "What a stupid creature; why would it come back three times more for the same punishment?" But then I thought, maybe he is more intelligent than I, for what my experiment proved was that he had more to fear from sharks in the sea than from a foolish scientist like me!

I found that there were very few species of plants, or should I say families of plants, for a few families had been transformed to adapt to the various terrains. The daisy, which most of us know as a small herbaceous plant, had grown into a tree like shrub. There were mockingbirds, relatives of the thrush or American robin, that had adapted to fill several different niches.

Most unusually, the finches were unique to each island. Some had adapted to eating seed and over time had developed larger beaks. Others had adapted to eating insects and had developed skinny beaks. One even learned to use a tool, a small stick, to extract insects from under bark. Of the 26 species of finches we caught, most were endemic or found on just a single island. Thankfully, the good captain had done a better job of labeling which island which birds came from because my collection was not so tidy. This discovery came to me after we had left the islands and were sailing across the Pacific. While I had time aboard the ship to look over this collection of unusual creatures, more questions arose:

What would cause the adaptation of a few species of plants and animals to fill each of these unique habitats?

What would cause them to change over time, to adapt? How does this adaptation aid in the survival of the fittest, natural selection, where some individuals survive to reproduce and others do not?

These questions began to haunt me as we sailed for weeks and weeks across the broad expanse of the Pacific Ocean towards Tahiti and Malaysia.

It was here on the open sea that I drew my first rough sketch of the tree of life. It was during that longest voyage that the answers to my questions began to fall into place.

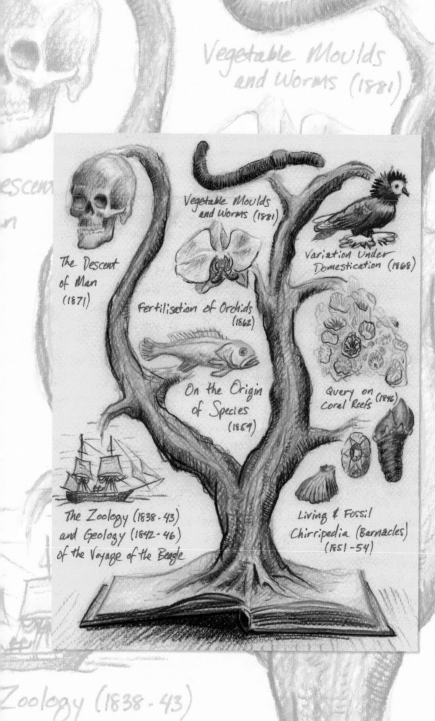

Charles Darwin and his Revolutionary Idea

HMS Beagle safely sailed into harbor October 2, 1836. I found to my astonishment that all of the specimens that I had sent home had made me a bit of a celebrity in the scientific community. Geologists wanted to study my collections of rocks, discuss the mountains of South America, and the formations of coral islands. Entomologists were eager to look over my collections of insects, beetles, butterflies, cicadas and katydids. Ornithologists wanted to see the birds. Ichthyologists wanted to have a look at the fishes. Botanists wanted to leaf through the plants. I was asked to lecture to various scientific organizations. I was even invited to be secretary of the Royal Geological Society. I published a book about my travels, *The Voyage of the Beagle*, which is still one of the best selling travel books ever written or so I am told.

I settled down. I married. My wife and I eventually had twelve children, and we created for ourselves a simple life on what was then the outskirts of London. Because my wife and I had both come from wealthy families with a large inheritance we were fortunate enough not to have to worry about our income.

I fell into a routine of family life, scientific research and publishing. Eventually, I wrote books about the breeding habits of barnacles, the orchids of the British Isles, the 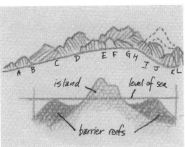 reproduction of worms, the formation of coral reef islands, and the geology of South America.

Because I wished to avoid the ridicule of the French scientist Jean-Baptiste Lamark and my grandfather Erasmus Darwin, I kept my ideas to myself. For thirty years I kept a secret notebook that I showed only to my closest friends.

I discussed my ideas on evolution with my colleagues and even went so far as to write a short scientific thesis, an article, that I showed only to the fellows I felt I could trust. They encouraged me to publish my ideas. I told them I needed more proof so the process was fully understood and irrefutable. They said this other work was  a distraction. I should focus on evolution. What they did not see was that ALL of this other work was all about evolution and working out the details of the process.

Then a young man who was collecting specimens in Polynesia, Alfred Russell Wallace sent me an article asking my opinion on his new theory of Natural Selection. I was astonished and heartbroken. In his article I found my theory virtually verbatim, even the headings of the sections of his article paralleled the titles of my chapters. As my friends had warned me, someone had stolen my thunder. But my friends, and truer friends one could not ask for, said it was out of my hands. They would take care of it. The ethical thing to do was to publish Wallace's article at the same time as my much more thorough treatment of the idea that several knew was written more than a dozen years earlier, giving my article some precedence. I then went to work on my now famous book, ***On the Origin of Species by Means of Natural Selection, Or the Preservation of Favored Races in the Struggle for Life***, now known simply as ***The Origin of Species***. The book sold out the first day! It went through several editions and is still one of the most controversial books ever written. Though I called it the long argument, I was loath to argue about it. I will let the truth stand the test of time.

What is the theory of evolution you might ask? Well, I have already laid out the evidence before you.

If you think about this theory of evolution through natural selection as my point of view or VISTA then maybe you can begin to understand how all of the answers are already there in my stories from the voyage of the Beagle. V.I.S.T.A. my view, stands for Variation, Inheritance, Selection, Time, and Adaptation.

V.I.S.T.A.

The Variation of species via the Inheritance of specific traits, through the process of natural Selection, over a broad expanse of Time, allows the Adaptation of individuals to evolve into new species.

I know my stories are a little out of order, but the scientific process, the process of making sense out of chaos, is sometimes a little disordered as well. But, the Variation of the rhea was a clue. The Inheritance of armadillos and sloths provided further proof. Natural Selection is happening everywhere, but where the broader diversity was swept away and one family of birds showed Adaptation to different islands in the Galapagos it became more clear that Time was a key factor. Here you have it, the evidence for the transmutation of species through the survival of the fittest, what is now called evolution.

Again, the words are a little out of order, but do you see my point of view, my V.I.S.T.A.? Let me tell you one more story to help make this clearer for you.

the Comet Orchid of Madagascar

Spur (3")

30cm (12")

On the tropical islands of Malaysia I found the most amazing species of comet orchid that had an unusually long spur or nectary, the chamber at the back of the flower that stores nectar. It was 30 centimeters long. I hypothesized that there must be a bird or butterfly that has a tongue or beak long enough to drink that nectar and pollinate the flower. Over time the tongue of the pollinator must grow longer, must adapt, to pollinate the flower or the flower would not produce seed, so its young could inherit the longer spur. This process of co-evolution where the tongue gets longer, meaning the pollinator is more successful, more fit to have young, and the variation of the flower, must grow hand in glove. Now some laughed at the idea that a bird or butterfly could have a foot long tongue. They used this one example in an effort to ridicule the entire theory. They said I must be making it up; if I can imagine an insect with a foot long tongue I could imagine anything. Fifty years later they discovered a sphinx moth that only lives in Malaysia that has a foot long proboscis that it carries curled up. This rare moth is the only pollinator for this rare orchid. It took them fifty years to find the evidence to prove this theory correct!

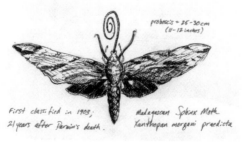

proboscis = 25-30cm
(11-12 inches)

First classified in 1903;
21 years after Darwin's death.

Madagascan Sphinx Moth
Xanthopan morgani praedicta

I knew that a large body of evidence would be required to convince the skeptics. I spent many years breeding fancy pigeons and rare flowers. I found that in a few generations, through man-made selection, I could radically change the appearance of a pigeon to give it the color of my choosing, add ruffles to the head, or add a larger fan tail. Yet, when I allowed them to breed on their own, within the fanciest variation of a pigeon, there were still the elements needed to breed back to the normal blue-grey rock dove, the one that we have all seen within our city parks.

My book, *The Origin of Species*, explains in great detail how organic forms are often replicated. Hold out your hand. If your fingers are stiff, pressed together, and all pointing forward you have the flipper of a dolphin. If you stretch your fingers and the skin between your fingers, you have the wing of a bat. If you elongate the smallest finger and reduce the rest you have the wing of a bird. If you cup your hand and grow your fingernails together you have a horse's hoof. Hoof, claw, feather and fingernail are all made of the same substance. All of these limbs, though each is adaptive to a different function, have an astoundingly similar form. Nature loves to re-use an idea.

As species are isolated by mountain ranges or vast stretches of the ocean or even the gulf between islands, over time, they adapt to subtle changes in the climate, changes in the food supply. The same changes that affect their prey or predators add further pressure to change. Because those that thrive survive, those that bare young successfully pass on those traits that are useful; these young survive and pass along those same traits. Those individuals that live at the edge of a population eventually become new species. Clearly, the fossil record shows that some species did not adapt and died out, while new species arise all of the time, over long periods of time. The evidence is apparent everywhere you look.

Now, I know there are some who will not change their minds no matter how complete the evidence. I also know that there are shortcomings to this theory. Having thought deeply for thirty years, I know these weaknesses better than most.

When some argue that the perfect pocket watch could not be randomly made by happenstance and ask us to look at the human eye as a perfect example of God's craftsmanship, I simply point to the light sensitive ganglia of the lowly worm, the multi-cellular light sensing pineal gland of sea creatures, the complex multifaceted eyes of dragonflies, and the eagle who has better sight than us as evidence that even something as complex as an eye can evolve with enough time.

When some ask about the holes in the fossil record, so called "missing links", I say we are just beginning to unearth the complete picture and as more fossils are found more proof will be revealed. One hundred fifty years of fossil findings have only strengthened the pool of evidence. I understand that recent discoveries of flying, feathered dinosaurs link them to modern birds. Fascinating!

When others argue about the role of God in all of this, I say that I am simply answering the mechanical questions about the origin of species; I will let the philosophical questions about the origin of the universe be answered by a theologian, someone more qualified to answer these questions than I. Yet the two of us do not have to argue because we are actually asking different questions, so of course we have different answers. Do not forget that I was studying for the clergy before I sailed around the world and took my Bible with me. One does not have to forsake God to be a scientist.

It is difficult to fathom that so many years after the publication of my book there are some still unwilling to believe what has become the foundation of all biological research. I am grateful that you have spent the time to listen to the proof instead of the hearsay. Your patience in listening to the ramblings of an old man has given me hope.

I remember writing a letter home to my sister from Tierra del Fuego, South America. I said that I could not employ my life better than in adding a little to our understanding of the Natural Sciences. This I have done to the best of my abilities. Critics may say what they like, but they cannot destroy this conviction.

My good friend from Illinois wrote me a wonderful letter affirming my ideas. Dr. Benjamin Walsh, the first American scientist to conduct his own research to confirm my theory said it best when he wrote, "Magna est veritas et veritas pravalebit - Great is the truth and the truth shall prevail!"

There have been so many discoveries since my time, homologous and convergent evolution, Gregor Mendel and genetics, the great synthesis of genetics and evolution where these two theories reinforce and add credence to each other. Teams of scientist have scoured the earth for 150 years since my book was published, and though my basic theory of evolution, transmutation through natural selection, has been refined and expanded, ALL of the evidence affirms this basic idea:

Through time species adapt to their environment and through natural selection new species arise.

Please, I invite you to imagine an entangled stream bank, clothed with many plants of many kinds; there are birds singing on the bushes, a multitude of insects flitting about, worms crawling through the damp earth, and this river cuts through layers of fossil plants and ancient sea beds. Reflect with me on these elaborately constructed forms; all have been produced by the laws of nature acting around us.

There is a grandeur in this view of life, Power breathed into a few forms or maybe just one, and while this planet has gone on cycling according to the fixed laws of gravity, from so simple a beginning, endless forms most beautiful and most wonderful have been and are still being evolved.

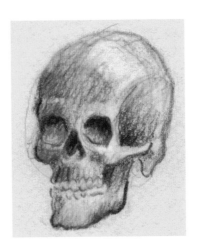

GLOSSARY – Evolution's Terms Defined

Evolution is easier to understand if you remember these key words:

V.I.S.T.A. = Variation, Inheritance, Selection, Time and Adaptation

The Variation of species via the Inheritance of specific traits, through the process of natural Selection, over a broad expanse of Time, allows the Adaptation of individuals to evolve into new species.

Variation – Within a species there are slight differences between individuals; these differences are called variations. For example, if you were to capture a hundred red foxes, you would notice that some have fur that is more orange, some are actually black, and some have a color pattern that looks like a cross on their back. Some might have shorter legs or longer legs. These slight variations might allow some to thrive and reproduce while others would be more likely to get eaten by a predator or they might have trouble catching their food.

Inheritance – With two parents, each parent gives half of their genetic material to their offspring creating a child, (or seed, or egg), that includes traits from both the mother and father, yet the offspring is unique. The kit, or baby fox, that is born with longer legs inherits this trait from his parents. But in a family of foxes maybe only two or three inherit this trait, maybe two foxes have longer legs and two have shorter legs.

Selection – Because there are many more offspring born than the natural world can support, some who are more fit to survive will thrive and create offspring. Those less fit will die; no offspring inherit these genes. In this competition for food and shelter, in this struggle to eat and avoid being eaten, nature selects the fittest. Natural selection is also called the survival of the fittest. So, the foxes with longer legs are better able to catch food and run away from their enemy.

Time – Long stretches of time, thousands of generations are required for new species to arise. Time is relative. For viruses and bacteria who reproduce dozens of generations in a few days they change, adapt, evolve much more rapidly than elephants, which takes 22 months to give birth. But over the course of hundreds of millions of years, individual species can slowly change to create new species. One red fox living in a desert will not change her color or grow larger ears to help her survive in this hot, dry climate, but over great periods of time and many generations, her great-great-great (times 10,000) grand-daughter might evolve or slowly change into a San Joaquin Kit Fox, especially if there is a mountain range that separates this group of foxes from all others.

Adaptation – As the earth changes, as climates change, animals change. These slow gradual changes are called **adaptations**. Eventually these adaptations, these gradual changes, add up and new species are created from the old. As foxes with short legs move out onto the prairie, their offspring with longer legs thrive, produce young, and this adaptation leads to a new species, the swift fox. As they move into the desert, those with larger ears, those who are better able to release heat and regulate their temperature will thrive. They produce young who inherit this trait and over great expanses of time, the desert kit fox evolves.

In North America we have several species of foxes, each have adapted to their unique ecosystem. Longer legs help the swift fox catch its food and avoid its predators in the open short grass prairie. Larger ears help the desert kit fox evaporate heat. Gray foxes have shorter legs and are the only fox that regularly climbs trees. These **Adaptations**, over great expanses of **Time**, have allowed these foxes to survive through natural **Selection**. So the traits are passed on to their young, **Inherited**, and what was once just a **Variation** within a species has eventually led to several new species.

Through time species adapt to their environment and through natural selection new species arise.

About the Text: My goal in putting together this book was to help make Darwin's brilliant ideas more easily understood by average folks who may or may not have a background in science. Much of the text is taken directly from his two books, ***Voyage of the Beagle*** and ***The Origin of Species***. If I have inspired you to read these books then I have accomplished my goal. The book is about 30-40% his words, direct quotes, another 30-40% paraphrased passages, and 100% Darwin. In complete humility I feel more like an editor than an author. I simply wanted to let Darwin speak for himself. All of the stories really happened and all of the ideas belong to him. All I did was to string it together in a way that I hope is entertaining and informative, updating Darwin's ideas for a modern audience. If I have succeeded, it is in large part due to the feedback I have received from my audiences as I perform my one-man show "Charles Darwin and the Voyage of the Beagle." Though this book is based on the script of my first person performance, it has been condensed and adapted for the world of print.

About the Author: **Brian "Fox" Ellis** - Since 1980, Brian "Fox" Ellis, storyteller, author and educator, has been touring the world collecting and telling stories. He performs a one man show as Charles Darwin originally commissioned by The Field Museum. He is a sought after keynote speaker and featured workshop presenter at dozens of conferences each year. He has also published ten books, including the children's picture book, *The Web at Dragonfly Pond*, winner of the Izaak Walton League's Conservation Education Book of the Year Award. His DVDs are some of the most award winning children's storytelling DVDs ever produced. He has written 20 musical theatre productions as the artistic director of Prairie Folklore Theatre. Fox works extensively as a museum consultant and he created a year-long position as the Storyteller in Residence for the Charlotte-Mecklenburg Schools. Please visit his web page for more information about booking a program:

www.foxtalesint.com

About the Artist: It has been several years since Peter Olson earned his MFA in printmaking from Northern Illinois University in DeKalb. Since that time he has been working as Preparator and Curatorial Assistant at the NIU Art Museum, where he was recently promoted to Assistant Director. Olson has participated in over 150 solo and group shows since undergraduate school at Ohio's Miami University. Within the recent past he has had several solo exhibitions in Illinois: in Bloomington, Evanston, Quincy, Oak Park, St. Charles, Elgin and DeKalb. Recent group exhibitions include the prestigious international Birds in Art in Wausau, Wisconsin (for three years in a row), American print surveys in Kansas and Indiana and a show at Chicago's Printworks Gallery. His drawings and woodcuts were featured in a three-person exhibition entitled Nature As Metaphor with several venues in the Midwest. Other professional activities include giving numerous lectures and printmaking demonstrations as well as contributions to national portfolios and journals. More of his work can be seen at:

www.peterolsonbirds.com

Charles Darwin and his *Revolutionary* Idea

2207912

Made in the USA